E

Contents

written by Pam Holden

A volcano is a mountain that has built up around an opening
in the Earth's surface. From deep inside the Earth, hot melted
rock, called magma, sometimes bursts out, pouring from the
mountaintop as burning lava, with steaming mud, gases, smoke
and ash. It can happen suddenly as pressure gradually builds up
inside until it explodes, or erupts.

sudden volcanic eruption

Most volcanoes are shaped like cones, but some are wide and flat, and some are under the sea or on islands. There are three types of volcanoes: alive, sleeping and dead.

- *Active* or live volcanoes may erupt suddenly without warning.
- *Dormant* volcanoes, which are sleeping, show signs of life, so might erupt again at some unknown time in the future.
- *Extinct* volcanoes have stopped erupting and are dead, so they are absolutely safe.

Active volcanoes are ready to blow up at any time. Whether an eruption is short or long, big or small, fierce or gentle, noisy or quiet, it can be extremely dangerous! Encircling the edge of the Pacific Ocean is a huge horseshoe shape called "The Ring of Fire". It is the home of more than 75 of the world's active and dormant volcanoes. Other places with active volcanoes are called "hot spots".

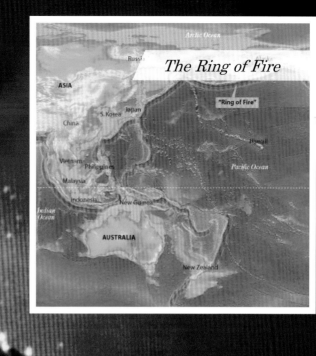

The Ring of Fire

Arctic Ocean

Russia

ASIA

"Ring of Fire"

S.Korea Japan

China

Hawaii

Vietnam

Philippines

Pacific Ocean

Malaysia

Indonesia New Guinea

Indian
Ocean

AUSTRALIA

New Zealand

The most active volcano on Earth is Mt. Kilauea in Hawaii, which has been erupting continuously since 1983. Red-hot lava pours into the sea constantly, making a spectacular sight, especially when observed at night!

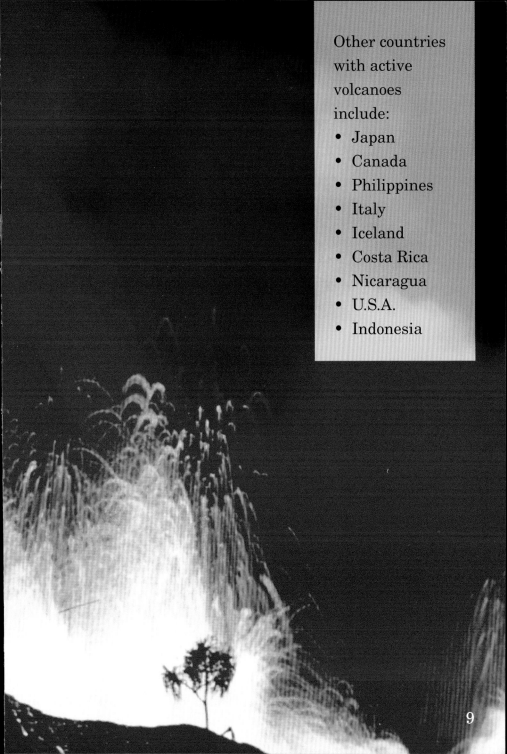

Other countries
with active
volcanoes
include:
- Japan
- Canada
- Philippines
- Italy
- Iceland
- Costa Rica
- Nicaragua
- U.S.A.
- Indonesia

An eruption on land brings great danger to humans and animals. Boiling lava flowing down a mountainside can reach farms, towns and forests, destroying lives as well as buildings and vegetation. Whole towns and villages have been buried in several parts of the world. Volcanic ash floating in the air is a serious danger to aircraft, as it limits visibility. It can also be sucked into jet engines, blocking them to a standstill.

incredible damage

11

We need special scientists called volcanologists who are trained to check volcanoes, sending warnings if there is any chance of an eruption. For safety on visits to observe volcanoes, volcanologists wear protective clothing and work with special equipment to measure volcanic activity. They collect samples of rock, lava and ash to study, so that more can be learned.

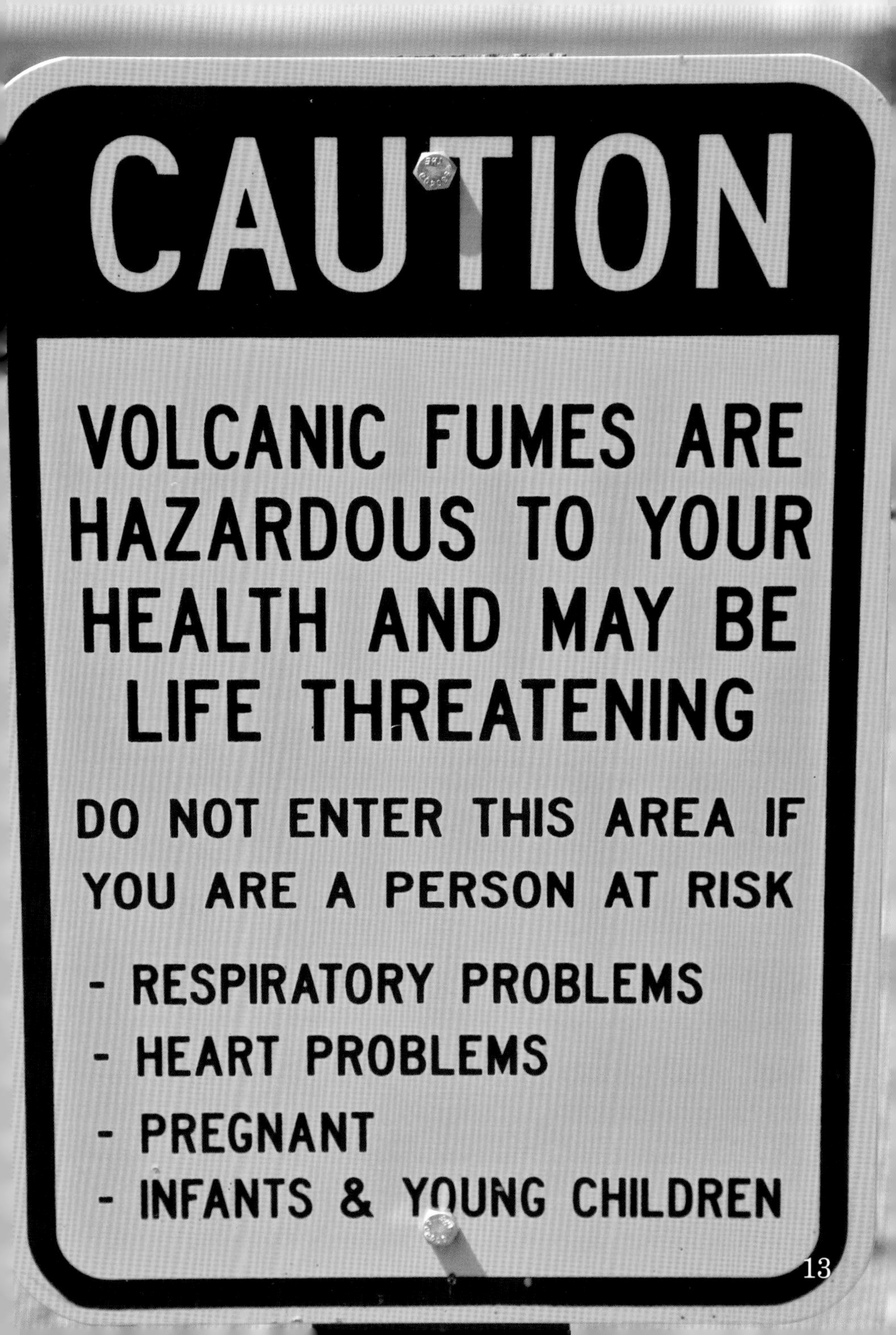

CAUTION

VOLCANIC FUMES ARE HAZARDOUS TO YOUR HEALTH AND MAY BE LIFE THREATENING

DO NOT ENTER THIS AREA IF YOU ARE A PERSON AT RISK

- RESPIRATORY PROBLEMS
- HEART PROBLEMS
- PREGNANT
- INFANTS & YOUNG CHILDREN

13

When we hear the word submarine, we usually think of a
ship that travels underwater. But there are many submarine
volcanoes that erupt on the sea floor. Boiling magma can push
an underwater mountain's cone up to the ocean surface where
it forms a new island. The islands of Hawaii were formed from
huge submarine volcanoes about a million years ago.

14

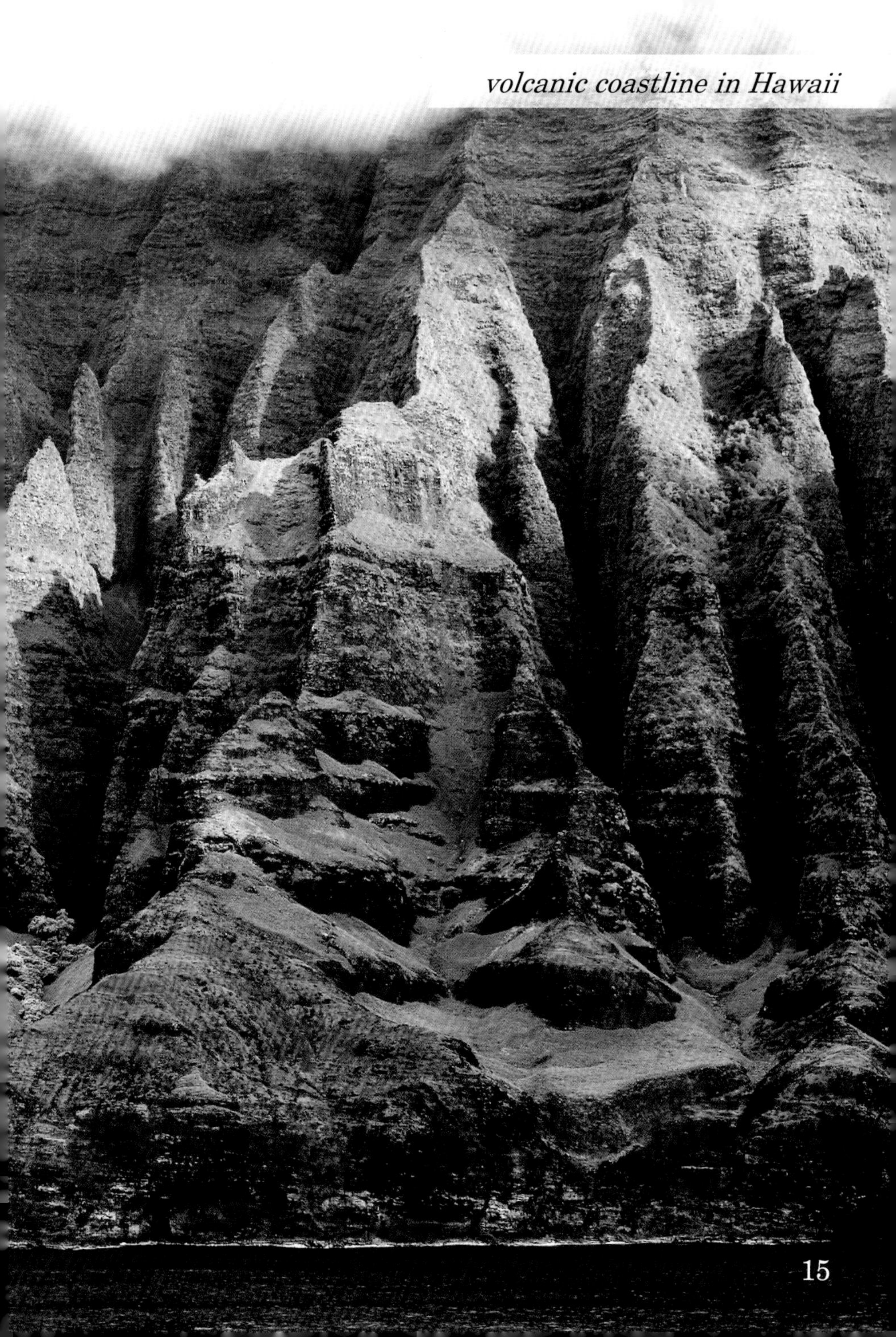

volcanic coastline in Hawaii

A mountain blowing its top is an amazing sight!
If we were close to an erupting volcano, we would see red-hot
lava pouring down the mountainside. We would feel enormous
heat, hear deafening roaring noises, and smell the black smoke.
We would be choking on the ash flying out of the fire as we raced
to save our lives. Being a witness to a volcanic eruption must be
a terrifying experience!

erupting volcano

Mt. St. Helens

A volcano that is not erupting is called *dormant*, which means "sleeping". It may be quiet for many years before awakening with an eruption that can be gentle or sudden, sometimes without warning, causing widespread damage and loss of life.

Mt. St. Helens in Washington State, USA, erupted in 1980 after being dormant for more than 120 years!

crater exploding

crater lake

Many volcanoes are *extinct*, which means that they are dead. They have stopped erupting and are safe, with no signs of life. Testing by volcanologists shows that they will probably never erupt again.

There are several useful things about old volcanoes. At the top of most volcanoes is a crater – a hollow which sometimes becomes a lake or grassy valley. Valuable gems have been found nearby, and miners have discovered copper, gold and silver there. Old lava thrown out years before becomes fertile soil for farming. Volcanic rock is useful to construct buildings, bridges and roads.

Active volcanoes are often visited at a safe distance by people wanting to see the amazing sight of lava streaming from an erupting mountain.

With the help of volcanologists checking carefully and giving warning of trouble, we can learn more about the wonder and power of volcanoes.